# I Bury What I Can't Bear

Harsh Dharmik

# OrangeBooks Publication

1st Floor, Rajhans Arcade, Mall Road, Kohka, Bhilai, Chhattisgarh 490020

Website: **www.orangebooks.in**

---

### © Copyright, 2024, Author

All rights reserved. No part of this book may be reproduced, stored in a retrieval system, or transmitted, in any form by any means, electronic, mechanical, magnetic, optical, chemical, manual, photocopying, recording or otherwise, without the prior written consent of its writer.

**First Edition, 2024**

**ISBN:** 978-93-6554-911-9

# I BURY WHAT
# I CAN'T BEAR

## HARSH DHARMIK

OrangeBooks Publication
www.orangebooks.in

*For all those who are insanely good at acting sane.*

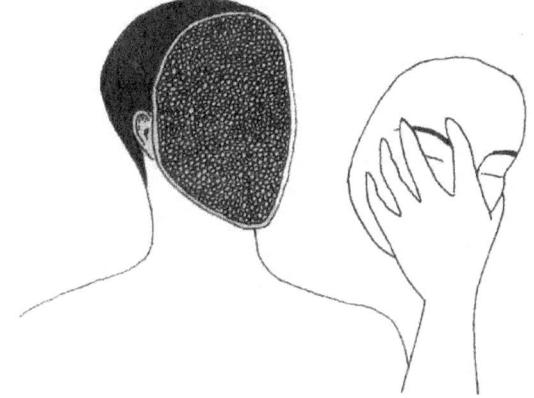

# **Preface**

I bury what I can't bear and yet it still fucking doesn't leave. All those things that I couldn't keep inside me, I put them down on paper in words.

They weren't always the things that were haunting me, but also the ones that were keeping me alive.

All these things broke my heart but I hope they heal yours.

# Contents

**Heartache** - For Someone I Once Thought I Loved.

**Void** - When all the love was gone...

**Hope** - For her, whom I will love forever.

**Fears** - Love made me realize...

**Madness** - I...

**Despair** - I always wished to be strong...

**Wretched** - Truths that hurt the most.

## **For Someone I Once Thought I Loved...**

---

I wrote I was in love, with the love I knew back then.

I was foolish but isn't that what love makes us?
I could see that whatever it was would soon end and destroy me.
But I wanted just something from her, even if it was painful.

I kept going back even when she kept on trying to push me away.

But when everything was going on, it all felt beautiful, even the pain.

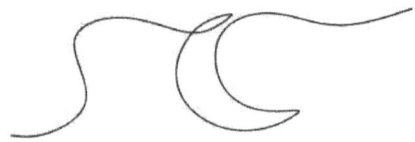

If I were to die before her,

I beg to whoever is in control -
God, Nature, Cosmos or the Ocean.

Please give my body to the moon.
I would reside in its corner.

So that when it glows at night
Her eyes look at me with glee in them.
And just like that,
I would feel more alive than ever.

I kissed your forehead before turning around and
walking away.

With time I created a city in my heart; by your name.

You were its only population
and its gates were forever closed
for anyone else.

Wrap a chain around my heart.

Push it in a cage or pierce a knife through the middle.
But somebody please stop it from breathing,

for I no longer want to hear her name every second.

I never missed someone this often,

someone other than you.

Someone I am trying to forget.

Even though this time,
time spent together was little,
And words said were few.

I believe that we both were aware that
*I was still not over you.*

I loved her in a way I wished someone would've loved me.
But was it the kind of love she craved for?
After all, it was all hers to experience.
She should've been the one to choose when and
how, how subtle or grey and
in what way she wanted to be loved.

So, I ask myself that even though I loved her,
Did she ever feel loved by me?

Because it's not about how much I loved her but
about how well I did.

With every hug that I gave you

I wanted to take a little bit of your pain away.

So, when we come to our last hug;

I would be the one to suffer and

you could smile more often.

## I Bury What I Can't Bear

I absolutely refuse to die if it's not any of these five ways.

First in a thunderstorm,
By the strength of the droplets falling on my heavy chest,
finally lifting the weight.

The second would be,
By falling from a mountain, my soul would keep smiling
every moment knowing I was a little closer to heaven before
finally going to hell.

Third might be a little painful but,
I think it would be my pleasure to drown in a sea and let
waves carry me wherever they wish to.

Forth has to be a slow poison
such as love or guilt.

Fifth, *by slowly yet deliberately drowning in her eyes.*

I have a soul that has drifted to its past.
Surviving there just to see her smile.

It watches those moments again and again,

and that's what keeps it *alive*.

## I Bury What I Can't Bear

And that's the beauty of my love.

She could rip my heart out if she wanted to,
Ravage my soul with those eyes.

She could shatter me to pieces if she wanted to.
And yet her every touch would still send
shivers down my spine.

She could close in the distance between us to wreck me,
and I would still smile at mere inches between us.

Is there really more?

So let me hear it

The love that I lost,

the dreams that I failed.

That time months ago when the world was ours.

I want another taste of what could've been,
So please just let me hear something other than a goodbye.

Because without you,
I don't think my heart will ever stop aching.

If I were to pen down a part of me;
pen down my laughter,
pen down my heartbeat,
pen down my tears.
If I were to write of my most beautiful thought

I would again write of her;

for she exists in all of it...

I Bury What I Can't Bear

When we held hands.
I wanted them to forget
that they were two separates.

I wanted them to remember
that the palm lines are no more alone.

For *they found their halves in yours.*

And yes, this is what I believe.

For I know that you and I will be a thing somewhere.

Either ahead in time or after it *ends*.

I Bury What I Can't Bear

The only thing that stands between me and my
happiness is my reality.

Because in reality, you are not mine anymore
even though I am yours *forever*.

And that's the gist of it.

While she remains in every inch of me,

I remain miles away from her thoughts.

## When all the love was gone...

---

After love was lost, I was lost too.
I wanted to wait but it would've killed me.
Whatever I wrote during all this time was my best
attempt at accepting reality and
moving on with my life.

Yes, it was tough but it was the most necessary thing
to do.

Sure, I can change stuff that reminds me of you.

I can decorate my times however I want

when I miss you.

The question is *would that erase your absence?*

You left your scent on my palms;

and a wound on my heart.

I no longer wish for butterflies in my stomach;

but rather for fireflies

in the darkest parts of my mind.

When everyone was rushing to love her more and more.

> She just needed someone to
> understand her a little.
>
> And when people *pretended* to
> understand me,
>
> I just needed to be loved a little.

I do not wish to be touched anymore.

I want to be held till eternity,

With your arms wrapped around my soul.

Just so it doesn't crumble again.

You were that one prayer I gave up *all* my wishes for.

You can never blame the sea,
because it drowned you.

It was your choice to sail.

You knew sea had the power to destroy you,

yet you still chose to sail,
yet you still chose to love.

## I Bury What I Can't Bear

I don't know what the hell will happen.

Yesterday I decided to fall in love again,

Today it all seems beautiful;

Though tomorrow I am scared it will hurt again.

Allow me to fall in love again.
Allow me to be a fool
and not know it.

Little delusional and frankly,
it feels humanly
to be in love once again.

When I look back,
I think that
*'Maybe I was born to smother you with love.'*

*You were nothing short of my everything.*

Sometimes when two people part,
*nothing* changes.

But nothing *remains the same* either.

## For her, whom I will love forever...

And just when I thought I would never fall in love again, my life turned different.

I fell in love again and this time it felt more like flying.

She taught me that love when it hugs you, won't hurt or crush you.
It will hold you gently.
So gently that you would never want to leave.

And that's exactly what loving her feels like.
I now know love as her.

I am no longer fluent in words.

I thought I was capable of poetry,
until my eyes witnessed the greatest poem

*That was you,*

And just when I was waiting for life to knock on my door;

I saw you tapping on the glass of my window.

## I Bury What I Can't Bear

The first time you caught my eye
It was not love at first sight.
Instead, a quiet curiosity was planted in my chest.

I knew that very soon
you would sink beneath my bones
and mix with my blood.

Flowing through me and keeping me alive.

It was just a matter of time
before you would make me question...

*If I had ever been in love before?*

I am where there falls sunshine at midnight.
Where the mornings are lazy
Where the nights are endless
Where the moon melts in the afternoon heat;
and butterflies know how to sing.

*I am in love.*

And I see your face in the clouds.
And you smell better than the after-rain.

Thunder clashes against your skin,
and you sound like a night breeze.

In this terrifyingly false world,
*You are the truest thing I know.*

In all ways, you are poetry material.

You are that one little bubble of all my favourite poems, The way you smell like autumn mornings, Green stardust in your eyes.
Your touch as delicate as a blue swallowtail wing

.

You are more poetic than the most poetic things.

All my knowledge of vocabulary faded,
sense of creativity melted,
poetic mind gave up and heart too knew
It would be of no help.

That's the effect you had on me.

That's the effect you have on me *still*.

Love is yellow, Love is irresistible.
Love is -

The sound of you and me whispering wishes,
pleasant sensation of your lips,
holding hands and writing a letter that will never end.

*Love is just a side effect of you...*

But I never knew light existed.

I thought home could be built in the darkness too,
but now that you have shown me light.

How could I live there in peace?

"Are you shivering?"

No, I am not.

"Yes, you are."

My world is coming to peace as I hug you.
It will take some earthquakes before it finally settles.

Have we met before?
It might feel strange
But it feels like,

*Our souls have laughed and danced together forever.*

If God has assigned all of us angels to protect us;
I would assign mine to protect your angels.

And my dear, if they fail

then I would send my devils too.

Your forehead against mine.
Your arms wrapped around my heart
Souls draped in the melody of our silence,
and your eyes looking into mine.

-Home.

I Bury What I Can't Bear

I sit here thinking how my heart sounds when we hug, that is only when it beats.

I know it wants to escape and I have captured it in a cage.

You are it's freedom love, even if it escapes someday it will run to you only.

Whatever it feels, it feels *because of you*.

I feel my heart burning at the moment.
Now that you've closed the distance between us,

I find it hard to breathe.

There are some days
when my heart is cold,
and my soul feels the chills.

It makes me shiver with fear.

These are the days when *you haven't hugged me tight.*

Believe me, there is no *Heaven* and *Hell*,

There is just your *Embrace* and your *Absence*.

Love is a tightrope we walk on.

Trying not to look down at
loneliness on one and tragedy on the other hand.

All I ask of you, my love;
is to keep your eyes looking ahead.

*Keep them on mine.*

What if our hearts are made up of clay,
mixed with the ashes of our past lovers.

And what if,
my heart was mixed with *yours*.

Say that instead of just white and black,
we blend in all our colours.

Paint a canvas for the two of us,
bleed on it a little,
and then

proceed to *build a home*.

You own me now.

Until the moment I remember,
How your lips feel on mine.

You own me forever.

I needed that breath you were holding in.
   I needed it more than anything else.

I kissed you because in that moment;
   I couldn't have done anything else.

I Bury What I Can't Bear

I can taste the universe on your lips.

I can taste every single one of your tears
that has died there.

So, with each kiss,
*I wish to steal them from you.*

I am sure love doesn't even come close.

It seemed too common,
too used and simple
for what I felt for you.

It's like everyone was in love
but..
*Me?*

I was in debt to the creator
for making my soul collide with yours.

*I was more than in love.*

I wish I could wrap my intestine around my neck.
I could feel something comfortable
warm and soft
like *your hands.*

I needed to witness your naked skin.

To hold the light from your radiating
body in my eyes for some time.

I needed to
Not touch you anywhere

But
Hold you everywhere.

I will undress your fear
like how fire undresses darkness.


I will set your guilt on fire
like how hatred sets alight kindness.

This freakishly quiet thing in me leaves,
at the sight of your raw naked skin.


I feel a need to growl your name,
worship your heavenly existence,
and fall on my knees at your touch.

Just what the hell is this love?

One moment I imagine us grinding our bodies together
and moaning each other's names.

At the same moment
I see my whole world in your eyes.

You touch me and I start to burn
But
At the same time, it keeps me warm.

One moment I want to be everywhere with
you and the same moment
I see us building a home.

I beg you not to differ
cause for me
Both are love.
And for me, all I know is that

*Love is you.*

Our bodies collide and our souls merge.

We speak a lot,
a lot more than words ever could.

*You are what flows through me and keeps me alive.*

So yes, there is you and me and a mirror between us.
You look at me and I look at you.
You see your misery and I see my helplessness.

But what if we break the mirror
and see each other.

I can praise your tries
and you can appreciate my gestures.

Your misery will be ours and
my helplessness will be gone.
You and me will be *us*.

The mirror can break if we both push it from the same side.
Let's not try alone, run alone, cry alone.

For once let's give ourselves someone too;
*Who is in the same sea and the same boat.*

I don't think I can live without you.

Without love?

I can.

But,

*I can't live without you.*

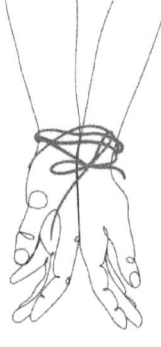

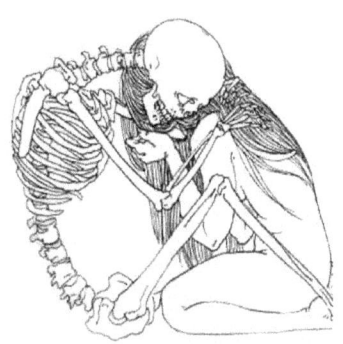

If you do decide to leave,
come back.

Even as a shadow,
Even as a dream
or a ghost.

But please come back.

There is not a single chance that I would've known you,
and not have fallen in love with you.

Even if I found out that your heart was on fire,
I would've still danced madly on its beats
until my feet burned.

## I Bury What I Can't Bear

What makes you so sure about her?

I am sure because even if someday she stabbed me with a knife
I would ask for the second blow to *be closer to my heart.*

Slowly I am starting to believe that -

She has no idea of how deeply she is incorporated into every idea of love I ever had.

## Love made me realize...

Love is also a lesson. Sometimes you learn how to love someone and other times you learn how to accept love.

Latter has always been tough for me but I now know it is most needed.

I was honestly okay in the dark,
totally okay.

But you were as bright as a shining light.

I wanted to stay close but I knew
I would pull you in the darkness too.

And so to change that,

I started *walking towards the light.*

I Bury What I Can't Bear

I never doubted you when you said you love me.

I never asked,

Do you still love me?

Cause I feared you would say no

I didn't want you to unlove me.

I wanted your love
even if it was not true.

Maybe I was drawn to you

because we drown in the same sea.

With just a few drops of love left in me
I learned to love you.

So, if you think I love you less
know that I am loving you with all that I have got.

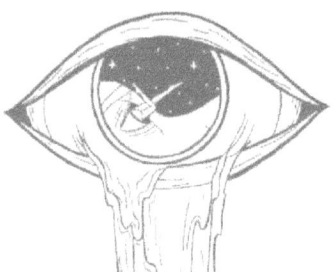

It was always in the eyes,
whatever I was trying to say.

Whatever it was that she never saw;

*it was always in the eyes.*

My breath sinks miles deep
right after you leave.

I feel like a *corpse*
with just air flowing through me.

Yeah, you are too much
you bleed a lot and everywhere.

You are too much for my arms to handle
Wait, let me wrap my soul around you.

And if someday you break my heart and kill me.

> I shall haunt you forever
> I shall capture any form
> and drive you mad.

But I shall never leave you alone in this abyss
*where I won't be able to love you.*

## I...

Has it ever happened that you started to know a lot about yourself but still you were unable to tell it to anyone properly?

Sometimes only you yourself know what's going on inside you and many times you want to explain it to people but you just don't know how to.

Wounded me desired nothing else
more than another wound.

A new one to cry about.

I wanna spend my time doing something

that prevents me from killing myself.

I just needed a couple of minutes to come back from the place my mind took me to.

It was pleasant.

Funny to think that
even though
I had no destination

*I am still lost.*

Other day I read something and went
'That sounds like something I would write.'

And then I thought
'What if I was the one who wrote it?'

What if I wrote it in my past life.

Then I smiled thinking
*How sad that I was miserable in my past life too.*

I say I am the greatest artist of all.

And what did I create you ask
I say I made a new myself;

*One that smiles.*

*But what if I am actually incapable
of tolerating my own heart?*

*What if skin to bone I am toxicated,
so much so that it's killing me.*

I could never get lost in poetry.
I get lost in this falsely real world.

But poetry is where I look for myself
and there is hope to find something.

Because I just can't;
really can't anymore
keep my breath in sync with the world.

If I were to destroy everything
that has ever been cruel to me.

I would begin with *myself*.

I Bury What I Can't Bear

I would lick my own heart when it flows out with pain,

I would eat my own brain,
before it bursts with guilt and kills me.

I won't let anyone destroy me.
If destruction is my fate, then I shall take over.
No one else but *me will destroy myself.*

What if I burn down a whole forest?

Will anyone come looking out for me?

If they see me burn,

Will they then get a *clue* of my suffering?

## I Bury What I Can't Bear

I wish something would break right now,

Like a knife
would fall from the sky
And pass through my skull.

You know I just had a thought,

What if my story was the one
which was supposed to be sad?

Like you know how some stories are,

They may have great plots, they are entertaining and
characters are interesting,
But nothing ever goes right and the ending
is *forever* sad.

# I Bury What I Can't Bear

But it's all-fake strength.

It's all a lie.
I lost a long time back
I am just faking another try.

I Bury What I Can't Bear

Tonight, I wish to sit naked,

break my clock

spray paint my room walls

and burn down my clothes.

I wish to pour some whiskey in a

glass and light it on fire too.

I think there is some misery happening.

What little love is left
is starting to leak out.

So, I put a tape on my lips
stopped breathing through the nose,
stopped listening to love speaking.

I was more scared of losing myself
a lot more than feeling love.

What did you dream?

I dreamt to be a myth.
One what's been heard everywhere.
One that's travelled far and wide.
One that's been to many places;
but does not belong to any.

I dreamt to be one such myth,
which even if you go looking for, has no traces of existence.

And now I wish this dream of mine to come true.
As I no longer want to move and still be everywhere.

I envy people those who have minds
that doesn't run far away searching for something.

And I pity the same people for the same reason.

How do I tell the ocean,
that I am drowning on the land too..

And just for a while,
I needed quietness

I was fed up with silence too.

## I always wished to be strong...

All that I have written here is my attempt to let my feelings go. You know how they say if you write about it then it gets lighter.

Well, that's what I tried but honestly, it never seemed to work for me.

The weight of papers started to crush my chest even more.

And what exactly do you write about
when it's all haze and smoke?
When thoughts are red?

What else can you do?
Except bleeding on paper.

I must be very wise to be able to
recognize my every emotion.

I must be very naïve to feel everything so deeply.

Okay, love filled the gap in my heart.

But what of this void in my brain?

Plant of loneliness is growing in there
and I am there to water it.

*I need someone to pluck it away.*

It's like I am always in a state of worry.
Even when I am in the moment
I am only *half* in it.

I can't let my feelings out.
> If I did them justice
> and let them out.
>
> *They would wreck me.*

Some people write, but some like me

vomit on the paper.

Poetry isn't always beautiful;

destruction isn't always artistic

Rust sometimes is just brown and not amber.

Nothingness is your biggest enemy in disguise.

It will surely turn down the noises.
But,
it will take away the music too.

It's either that I am stupid
Or
The whole world is speaking a foreign language.

You say you want an elaborative answer.

How could you possibly not understand something as simple as,

'I am not okay.'

I was done; almost
done with gathering pieces of my heart back.

I was done; almost
done picking myself up from the floor

I was done; almost
done with cursing myself for making bad decisions.

I was done; almost
done with living lies.

I was almost out of the dark
almost into the light again.

I was *almost* okay.

I Bury What I Can't Bear

And I wonder if love knows

that I have always been

begging for its arrival.

I was waiting for people to love me,
They were waiting for me to let them

                              -I am scared of love.

What consumes my mind mostly
troubles me the most.

I don't know what it is.
A part of me that harms me

Consumes me
From within.

One where my words do not form as desired.
One where I cannot smile very often.
One where tears do not fall
And I don't even bother to react.

I think I like that feeling;
the feeling of nothing.

Cause lately all I feel is nothing.

Loneliness wraps around my head,
and guilt wraps around my heart.

It takes a lot more than oxygen and blood
for me to be normal.

Just for tonight let the pain slip away;
while I lay in the lap of moonlight.

Let my tears justify me being strong for all this while
because I have to be strong again tomorrow
when the sun shines.

Still there is this strong desire to run away
Still there is this stronger one to take you along
And yet again the strongest is the guilt of disappearing.

I think I will forever be lonely.

I fear loneliness has become a part of me or even worse

I have become a part of the loneliness.

I liked the melancholy of things.
Sadness suited me.

And when I was sad; I easily recognized myself in the mirror.

I am homesick for a home,
I am not sure even exists.

At least I have a comfortable chair to sit in,

I wouldn't mind dying in this position...

The sight of the afterlife had never been clearer than ever today.

It's like I can almost taste death;
and surprisingly it's not bitter.

But rather very tempting.

## Truths that hurt the most...

There are things that we learn after going through hell and we always have a hard time accepting them completely.

We sometimes wish we didn't know them and hope that the pain they brought could be erased.

I Bury What I Can't Bear

Tonight, I feel like
I want to burn the world for the first 7 minutes.

Then for the next 11 ; I want to watch it burn.

But for the last 2
I want to pretend
that I am trying to
save it.

Why you ask,
Simply because that's what the world did to me.

There's not much to say.
No,
There's so much that I don't know where to start.

Say, I knew where to start from;
The problem would be two things:
One, I wouldn't know when to stop.
I would have to control myself from screaming constantly.

There is this desire to shut out the world.

Even the people you love
Even the people that love you.
*Especially* the people that love you.

And what was once lost is still missing.

I don't blame the world anymore
I take all of it on myself.

So, if you think it's funny,
Feel free to laugh at my misery.

Will happiness ever arrive?
Even in disguise.

Whatever you think lie ruins,
Do you think the truth could've saved it?

And since when does silence start to appeal more to me than words?

You can talk about what hurts you
but never about what breaks you.

How could I trust beautiful places to make me feel good?
When I only cried even in my mother's arms.

They wrote about monsters with human faces;
instead of angels in human bodies.

Still, I kept reading.,

There's a poem written underneath my tongue; you might never hear it.

But it is there.

Say that my ears are blind
and eyes are dumb.

I do not know where to see;
Neither can I know the true meaning of words.

I only hear what pleases my heart
and look at things the easy way.

And everyone around me seemed so familiar with themselves.

They knew a lot more than just their

name, age, likes and dislikes.

Unlike me who had a different name even for my inner child.

There is no such thing as your true self.

We partly are the movies we watch;
The books we read
The songs we listen to,
The food we like and the people we love.

Most of these change with time.
So how can one expect someone to stay the same always?

Fall they said, break down they said.

You will learn a lesson, they said,

You will become wise, they said.

But I don't think any amount of wisdom is worth that pain.

Don't choose the wrong route in hopes of learning.

What is meant for you to learn will come to you

on any route that you choose.

You say you want to get to know me.

You can try all you want;
but my heart and mind are different beings.

You can't make a sane being out of them.

I Bury What I Can't Bear

My reality leaks from my dreams.

It spreads over my sheets

and I can't wrap it around me when I am asleep.

No, I don't want to read another sad quote and relate to it.

I don't want anyone else to write my story.

I claim my right to feel my pain and feel it entirely.

Don't you dare paint my canvas red,

Maybe I want it black.

Some people you can never unlove because
all that you know about love
is because of them.

No devil can be as cruel as a human being.
Who is so artistically, so sugar-coatingly cruel,
Devils when they sin, sin with pride.

Oh yeah, that's right...

I kept on thinking about life

instead of *living* it.

And the world always laughed at me for dancing,

Even though they could never listen to the music...

## **Acknowledgment**

Writing a book is a lonely journey.

But when it comes to publishing it then it's a whole different story.

My parents always supported me to do it and I take this as an opportunity to thank them.

Especially my Baba.

The team of orangebook publishers helped me get my work out there, I want to thank them for that.

But there is someone without whom this book wouldn't be what it is today.

A huge thanks to you Pragya Mundra, for all that you did.

Right from designing the front cover, suggesting the illustrations, and editing the drats like a hundred times.

Sure I wrote this book but you made it what it is today.

www.ingramcontent.com/pod-product-compliance
Lightning Source LLC
LaVergne TN
LVHW061548070526
838199LV00077B/6958